MONGOLS

Galadriel Watson

WEIGL PUBLISHERS INC.

Published by Weigl Publishers Inc.
350 5th Avenue, Suite 3304, PMB 6G
New York, NY 10118-0069 USA
Web site: www.weigl.com

Library of Congress Cataloging-in-Publication Data

Watson, Galadriel Findlay.
  Mongols / Galadriel Watson.
     p. cm. -- (Indigenous peoples)
  Includes index.
  ISBN 1-59036-220-9 (lib. bdg. : alk. paper) 1-59036-257-8 (softcover)
  1. Mongols--Juvenile literature. I. Title. II. Series.
  DS19.W38 2005
  951'.7--dc22
                              2004005772

Printed in the United States of America
1 2 3 4 5 6 7 8 9 0   08 07 06 05 04

Project Coordinator Heather C. Hudak **Design** Terry Paulhus **Layout** Katherine Phillips and Jeff Brown **Copy Editor** Donald Wells **Photo Research** Wendy Cosh and Ellen Bryan

Consultant Richard K. Hines, Ph. D.

CONTENTS

Where in the World?

Mongolia is located in East Asia. Russia borders Mongolia to the north, and China borders it to the south, east, and west. Mongolia is 604,829 square miles (1,566,500 square kilometers) in size.

On the **steppes** of central Asia, groups of people called Mongols roam the land with herds of cattle, sheep, goats, camels, and oxen. Their favorite animals, horses and dogs, work alongside the people.

The term "Mongol" refers to many tribes, such as the *Khalkha*, the *Ordos*, and the *Buryat*, who have a closely related history and culture. The Mongols's homeland is a large stretch of land that includes mountain ranges, grasslands, lakes, rivers, and the Gobi Desert. This land is now divided between China and Mongolia.

Mongolia is the Mongols's native country. Almost all the people who live in Mongolia are Mongols. In China, Mongols live in the Inner Mongolia Autonomous Region of China. However, Inner Mongolia is home to only a small population of Mongols. Other Mongols live

throughout China and in nearby countries such as Russia.

Traditionally, the Mongols are a nomadic people. This means they travel often, moving their herds in search of grass or to escape harsh weather. The Mongols are also known to take part in wars. For centuries they fought among themselves and with other countries.

In addition to herding, the Mongols hunt wolves that threaten their herds of sheep and cattle.

As a result, in the thirteenth century, the **Mongolian Empire** stretched across Asia and into Europe. It was the largest **contiguous** empire in history.

Today, the Mongols are peaceful people. Only a small percent of the Mongol population remains nomadic. About half of all Mongolians make their homes in towns and cities. About one-quarter live in Mongolia's capital city, Ulaanbaatar. Those remaining in the country often work on large ranches. Still, most Mongols enjoy the freedom of being outdoors, a feeling expressed in the Mongol saying, "Man's joy is in wide open and empty spaces."

- Mongolia covers an area of 604,829 square miles (1,566,500 square kilometers). This is about the same size as Alaska. Mongolia has a population of 2.4 million people. This is about the same population as Utah.

- The word *Gobi* is a Mongolian word that means "desert." The Gobi Desert, divided between Mongolia and China, is almost as large as Mongolia itself.

- Mongolia has more than 1,200 rivers, 200 glaciers, and 4,000 lakes.

- In Mongolia, there is much more **livestock** than humans. In fact, there are about 12 times more animals than people.

Stories and Legends

Most Mongols believe in one of two religions: shamanism or Lamaism. Shamanism, the Mongols' oldest religion, claims the spirit world is present in nature. The god of the heavens, Tengri, is in the sky. This is why Mongols believe bright blue, the color of the sky, is a lucky color. The goddess Itugan, controller of plants and animals, rules Earth. Erleg Khan rules the lower world beneath the ground. Other spirits control other aspects of nature.

Mongolian priests are called shamans. It is the

Mongolian myths usually explain aspects of the natural world. They explain the creation of the world, animals, stars, and planets. Stories also tell about the struggle between good and evil.

shaman's job to speak with spirits. The Mongols believe spirits help cure illnesses, drive away evil, or find lost animals. Followers of shamanism are **superstitious**. For example, they believe that men who leave on long trips should sprinkle milk on their **stirrups** as a blessing. Mongols also believe both water and fire are sacred. The Mongols believe water, such as springs and rivers, represent gods. They believe it is a sin to pollute the water. This explains why, in the past, Mongols rarely

washed themselves or their clothes. They believed these activities would anger the gods. It also explains why water was not used to put out fires. Instead, the Mongols carefully removed the stones to release the fire. The Mongols used fire to **purify** things.

Lamaism was introduced to the Mongols during the height of the Mongolian Empire. It is a form of **Buddhism**. Named for the lamas, or Buddhist priests, Lamaism encourages followers to have faith in three things. The first is Buddha, a man from ancient Nepal. It is believed Buddha discovered why life is full of suffering and how people can escape this suffering. The second is the "Four Noble Truths," which suggest that people can stop suffering by separating themselves from material items. To do this, people must follow the "Eight Fold Path." This means people should have kindness, purity of heart, truthfulness, charity, and avoid fault-finding, envy, hatred, and violence. The third is the *sangha*. The sangha is the Buddhist community, particularly the community of lamas.

Buddhist monasteries are places where a group of religious people, such as monks, live. Here, religious dances called *tsam* were performed during annual ceremonies. These dances symbolized the protective power of the Buddhist faith.

THE STORY OF THE MORIN-KHUUR

Long ago, a young man named Sükhe found a foal, or young horse, beside its dying mother. Over the years, Sükhe raised the foal with great care. One day, he entered the animal in a horse race. Sükhe and the horse won the race. Unfortunately, this meant they defeated all nine horses of the area's governor, an evil man who became very angry.

That night, Sükhe found another dying horse. This time it was his own beloved horse, shot with several arrows. Struck with grief, Sükhe fainted. However, he met his horse again in his dreams. The horse instructed him to create an instrument, a type of fiddle, using the dead horse's hair as its string. This instrument is called the morin-khuur. When played, it has a sad sound.

Today, the Mongols can still feel Sükhe's love and sorrow when they play the morin-khuur.

Out of the Past

Four turtles guarded the four entrances to the city of Kharakhorum, which Genghis Khan declared the capital of the Mongolian Empire. Sculptures from this era are rare.

Archeological evidence shows humans have lived in the Mongols's homeland for 700,000 years.

Throughout history, the Mongol culture has alternated between periods of tribal warfare and peaceful unity. The Mongolian Empire is the most famous period in Mongol history.

Genghis Khan, also known as Chinggis Khan, became khan, or ruler, in 1206. During his rule, Genghis Khan took control of all the Mongol tribes. Then, he waged war on countries to the north, south, east, and west of Mongolia. Throughout the thirteenth century, the empire grew. By the time Genghis Khan's grandson Kublai Khan was in power, the empire was at its largest, stretching across Europe and Asia, from Hungary to Korea and Siberia to Tibet.

Kublai Khan was Genghis Khan's grandson. He ruled Mongolia from 1260-1294. He allowed his subjects to keep their religion and culture. He was famous for his luxurious palace at Xanadu.

Although they were great warriors, the Mongols were not great administrators. **Bureaucrats** ruled the empire and started gaining power. Cultures within the empire were too different to be united. Mongol tribes kept fighting. As a result, the empire began to break up into smaller kingdoms. By the late 1300s, the empire was nothing more than the area now known as Mongolia and a few scattered areas. Soon, the Mongols returned to their way of life as warring tribes.

In the 1600s, another culture, the Manchus, gained control over Mongolia and China. The Manchus divided the land into two areas: Inner Mongolia and Outer Mongolia. Today, Inner Mongolia remains part of China. This area practices Chinese culture. China ruled Outer Mongolia until 1911. At this time, the Mongolians rebelled and gained control from the Chinese rulers. After a short rule under Russian **troops**, Outer Mongolia finally became the nation of Mongolia in 1921. Soon after, the Soviet Union gained control of Mongolia and Mongolia became a **communist** country. After the Soviet Union broke up in the early 1990s, Mongolia became a **democratic** country.

TIME LINE

700,000 years ago People live in the Mongols's homeland

1206 Genghis Khan becomes khan. The Mongolian Empire is created

1227 Genghis Khan dies

1264 Kublai Khan, Genghis Khan's grandson, becomes khan. The empire stretches across Europe and Asia, from Hungary to Korea and Siberia to Tibet

Late 1300s The Mongolian Empire breaks up

1634 Manchus take over Inner Mongolia

1691 Manchus seize Outer Mongolia

1911 The Mongols drive the Chinese from Outer Mongolia

1921 Mongolia declares independence

1991 The Soviet Union breaks up

1992 Mongolia becomes a democratic country

Social Structures

and cattle were stolen from other clans.

Clans formed the basis of Mongolian nomadic life. Clans traveled together, moving to a new place when the herd needed new grazing land or during cold weather. Clans closely associated with one another were a tribe.

Work was divided between men and women. It was the man's job to take care of the horses, the Mongols's most prized possession. Boys learned to ride horses, make saddles and **bridles**, milk **mares**, and make bows and arrows. Girls also learned to ride horses, cook, make clothes, milk cows and goats, and make *yurts*, or felt tents. Women cared for all animals except horses. Both men and women could offer opinions about important issues. Women were sometimes warriors and khans.

In the past, parents arranged marriages. Boys usually married when they were 17 or 18 years of age. Girls married when they were about 15 or 16 years of age. Wedding preparations could take as long as 3 years. The wedding celebrations lasted 3 days. Today, however,

Mongol camps are usually made up of a circle of yurts belonging to members of an extended family.

Mongols traditionally lived in family units. These units had a husband, one or more wives, and their children. Several families were grouped into **clans**, or *oboks*. Most of the men in a clan were related. The wives came from different clans. Sometimes, women, horses,

Caring for herds is an important part of family life in Mongolia. Families move their yurts often so that livestock can have access to a good source of food and water.

Mongolians choose their own partners, and divorce is becoming more common.

Many unspoken rules guide Mongol life. For example, Mongols point with all fingers—to use just one finger is considered rude. Mongols do not stare into the eyes of an elder, and women cover their mouths when laughing. Both hands should be used when accepting food or gifts. A yurt is always open to any hungry, tired traveler, even if the owner is not at home.

THE SEASONS

Mongols have to deal with extreme heat and cold. The short, hot summers can be as warm as 96° Fahrenheit (36° Celsius). Temperatures reach 113° F (45° C) in the Gobi Desert. Winter is long and severe, with temperatures falling as low as -62° F (-52° C). There is never much snow or rain.

Communication

Mongolian is the official language of Mongolia. Mongolian is a language made up of many **dialects**. Khalkha Mongolian is the official dialect.

There was no written form of the Mongolian language until Genghis Khan became ruler. During his rule, Genghis Khan wanted to write down his laws. He commanded his sons to learn the writing system of one of their prisoners, a Uyghur Turk. The resulting text was made up of squiggly lines laid in top-to-bottom columns. The oldest Mongol book is *The Secret History of the Mongols*, which profiles Genghis Khan's history. Since then, the Mongols have tried many other writing systems, but none have been successful. After Mongolia came under Soviet influence, the Russian Cyrillic became the official Mongolian alphabet. However, this alphabet does not successfully represent some of the Mongolian sounds.

Today, many people are returning to the traditional Uyghur script, which is now being taught in schools.

Stories have always been a popular form of Mongolian communication. Tales of adventure on the steppes have been passed down from generation to generation. Professional singers have always traveled with and entertained the nomads with detailed stories.

Today, Mongolians use many forms of

Today, Mongol children attend schools where they learn new ways to communicate through second languages and computer skills.

communication. They can read about current events in dozens of newspapers, and radio has been available since 1931. About one in every twenty Mongols own a television. This television receives both local and **foreign** broadcasts from satellite connections. In the capital city, Ulaanbaatar, companies provide Internet and e-mail access.

As for traveling, there are thousands of miles (km) of roads crossing Mongolia, although most are made of dirt. Railroads link Mongolia with Russia to the north and China to the south. Mongolian Airlines carries both passengers and freight.

Today, many Mongols use modern transportation, such as bicycles, to help them get from one place to the next.

MESSAGES

In 1234, Genghis Khan wanted to develop a way to communicate with his army while it was at war. Since his army was in many different places, he needed a reliable method for sending them messages.

The answer was the *urtuunii alba*, or postal service. Similar to the United States' Pony Express, the Mongolian system used horseback-riding couriers. Stations were maintained at precise intervals along specific routes. This allowed the couriers to feed, rest, and exchange tired horses. All herders had to work for the postal system for 45 days each year, as well as provide horses. This postal system was so successful it continued until radio and **telegraph** arrived in Mongolia in the mid-1900s.

Law and Order

When Mongol clans joined together as tribes, the tribe was named after the strongest clan. Weaker clans kept their leaders and herds, but they had to submit to the will of the strongest clan. The tribe leader was called the khan. A successful leader could persuade men to leave their own clans to join his clan. The men who left their clans were called *nokers*. Tribes also allied with one another, usually in an attempt to prevent attack from other tribes. During a period of tribal meetings called "All the Mongols," Genghis Khan united Mongolia and began creating the Mongolian Empire.

Before Genghis Khan became ruler, laws were based on custom. There was no alphabet with which to write laws. Once Genghis Khan introduced the Uyghur alphabet, laws could be put into words. The new code of laws was called the *Yassa*. The Mongols strictly enforced the Yassa. People who broke the law were often harshly punished. Other countries ruled by the empire also had to obey these laws, although

Genghis Khan's accomplishments were recorded through art. A Persian story titled *The History of the Mongols* shows Genghis Khan's army storming the Tangut fortress.

they could keep their own religions and other aspects of their cultures.

In 1911, when the Outer Mongolians drove out the Chinese, the law was enforced by the lamas. The head of the Mongolian Tibetan Buddhist Church was proclaimed khan of all Mongolia and dubbed "the Living Buddha." However, Mongolia's tie with the Soviet Union changed this situation. Communism shuns religion, and Mongolia's new communist government closed monasteries, took their herds and land, and convinced many lamas to give up their religious lives. In 1924, there were 100,000 lamas in Mongolia. In 1990, there were only 110.

Mongolia's communist government was called the Mongolian People's Revolutionary Party and was the only party allowed to rule. By the 1990s, however, Mongolian citizens were demanding more freedom. The first free elections were held in 1990, and Mongolia became a democracy in 1992.

Today's laws are a blend of Russian, Chinese, and Turkish laws. The Great State Hural is Mongolia's **parliament**. Voters elect a president every 4 years,

and a prime minister carries out everyday operations.

The country is divided into 21 provinces, or *aimags*.

Today, there are more than 100 Buddhist monasteries in Mongolia.

Celebrating Culture

Mongols celebrate many special occasions. They celebrate a child's first haircut. The hair-cutting ritual takes place when a child reaches 4 to 5 years of age and the dangers of infancy have passed. The Mongols celebrate weddings and the **branding** of young horses. They also celebrate the Lunar New Year, or *Tsagaan Sar*. This celebration marks the end of winter and beginning of summer. Tsagaan Sar takes place in January or February. To mark the Lunar New Year, Mongols gather at relatives' homes for a special meal of *buuz*, or meat dumplings. The Mongols offer milk or *airag*, the national beverage, to the spirit of the sky. They also greet each other with good wishes.

The biggest celebration is *Naadam*. This annual festival began in 3,000 BC. Today, Naadam is held on July 11 every year. During this festival, tribes gather together to compete in strength, shooting, and riding categories. These are the skills necessary to be a great warrior. Wrestling, **archery**, and horse racing are called the Three Games of Men. Men compete in these sports during the festival.

More than 1,000 wrestlers compete at the largest Naadam gathering, which takes place in Ulaanbaatar. Mongol boys are taught to wrestle at a young age. They learn that the correct

Special songs are sung to praise the winners of Naadam.

stance combines the posture of a lion and the outspread wings of a bird in flight. Unlike international wrestling, which takes into account differences in the competitors' heights and weights, all Naadam wrestlers are considered equal. Winners earn titles such as Lion, Elephant, or Falcon. A three-time winner is called a *Darkhan Avraga,* or "Invincible **Titan**."

Archers use ancient bows and arrows to shoot at leather-covered targets. They compete for titles such as Miraculous Archer or Most **Scrupulous** Archer. Traditionally a man's sport, archery is now involving more women.

In Mongol society, children learn to ride a horse almost as soon as they can walk. Children compete in the Naadam races. Children 5 to 12 years old, dressed in traditional Mongol costumes, race from 10 to 20 miles (16 to 32 km) across country. They often ride bareback. The distance the child must travel is determined by the horse's age. They usually travel the distance between two *urtuunii alba* postal stations. Children ride in the horse races because lightweight **jockeys** show the horses at their best.

Horse trading is an important part of festivals such as Naadam. Horse races test the horse's skill as much as they test the rider's skill.

Art and Culture

The oldest art forms in Mongolia was created during the Bronze Age, or about 3000 BC. This art is called "reindeer stones." These are rock blocks carved with Sun, Moon, deer, tool, and weapon shapes. These rocks were probably used as markers for sacred sites or graves.

Mongols have always produced many arts and crafts. Their carved, wooden chess sets are known throughout the world. The Mongol chess sets substitute khans for kings, dogs for queens, and camels for bishops. The Mongols adorn yurt entrances with *shirdegs*, or detailed felt carpets. They also decorate pottery with fancy designs. Everyday objects are beautifully crafted. For example, silver enhances knives, belt buckles, and bridles. **Needlework** adorns clothing, shoes, and saddles. Yurt furniture is decorated with detailed patterns. Even tools are works of art.

The Mongols's talents also extend to architecture. Although they were nomadic, there is still evidence of ancient towns, temples, and monasteries. The most notable building is the palace of Ögödei, Genghis Khan's son. The palace was decorated with gold fountains in the shape of elephants, lions, and horses. Another palace, built in 1898, now houses the Palace Museum and its collection of Mongolian folk art.

In the sixth century, the Mongols began carving statues of people, complete with clothes, weapons, and tools. Painting began in the

Saddles are made with great care and attention to detail. Beautiful saddles reflect the status and origin of a rider.

eighth century. The Mongols used mineral and vegetable dyes to paint on cloth, which was often framed in **silk**. The Mongols often used appliqués, or pictures created by sewing together pieces of silk and other fabric, in religious art.

Today, Mongolians embrace many art forms. There are many types of theaters, including those for drama, opera, and ballet. There is also a puppet theater and a national circus. Rock bands perform at Naadam festivals, and Mongolian films are being shown at international film festivals. There are also many museums and libraries.

ARTISTIC ATTIRE

Mongols wear clothing styles that, while similar to some other cultures, are completely unique. Making these clothes is an art form that has been practiced for centuries.

Most Mongols have special forms of traditional clothing for different events. The more decorative the clothing, the more important the event. Different Mongol communities are identified by the color, shape, and decoration of their clothing.

Mongols added embroidery, appliqués, and stitched felt art to their clothing.

Mongolian artists sell their handicrafts to tourists and others at outdoor markets during the summer months.

Dressing Up

During the Soviet period in Mongolia, traditional dress was replaced by Western clothing. Today, traditional clothing is popular among rural nomads and for special occasions.

Mongol clothing must meet many requirements. It must protect against sweltering heat and bitter cold. Clothing must be comfortable enough to allow a person to move freely, particularly on horseback. It must be compact and portable so that it is easy to transport from camp to camp. A person away from home must be ready for any weather condition.

For both men and women, the main piece of clothing is a *del.* Like a long coat or robe, the del crosses over the front and buttons down the side to keep out drafts. A large sash serves as a belt and a place to hang small items such as a **flint** or chopsticks. Mongols wear an undershirt beneath the del. They also wear a sheepskin or fur lining in winter. On the coldest days, Mongols may wear an additional layer on top of the del. The del's long sleeves can be rolled down and worn like mittens. Heavy pants keep the Mongols' legs warm.

Mongols wear leather boots to protect their feet. Specially designed with an upward-pointing toe, these boots leave plenty of room for thick felt or wool socks while still allowing air to circulate and remain warm. The boots also will not get caught in the stirrups if a rider falls off his or her horse.

Hats are important for warmth, protection from the Sun, and as a sign of respect. For example, Mongols must wear a hat to greet people.

There are many different types of hats. Mongols wear hats for different occasions. They wear felt caps in summer and fur caps with earflaps in winter. Hats are often decorated with feathers, precious stones, buttons, spikes, or tassels.

MAKING FELT

Many Mongol items, such as yurts, rugs, saddle pads, and some clothing, are sewn from felt. To make felt, the Mongols beat sheep's wool. This mixes and loosens the fibers. Then, they place the wool in layers on an old piece of felt. They soak the layers with water and sprinkle grass on top to prevent the layers from sticking together. Then, they roll up the layers, soak the roll with water, and tie it together. Two people on horseback pull the roll back and forth. With enough force, the fibers join, compress, and lock together. This creates a new layer of felt. The felt is watered once more and allowed to dry. This shrinks the felt to make it more dense and durable.

Upper-class Mongolian women were often known for wearing elaborate hair styles and accessories.

Food and Fun

Animals provide food, clothing, shelter, and transportation. Their waste is used as fuel for heating and cooking fires.

Meat and milk are the two main components of the Mongols's diet. Most of their meat comes from herds of cattle, sheep, and goats. The Mongols may also hunt wolves, rabbits, deer, or other wildlife. Mongols eat horse meat on rare occasions.

Boiled **mutton** soup is a favorite Mongolian meal. However, the national dish is buuz, or mutton dumplings. Another dish, *khuurshuur*, is a pancake made of flour and mutton. Meat is preserved for the winter in thin, sun-dried strips or in dried sausages. All parts of a **slaughtered** animal are used, from the meat to the lungs, heart, stomach, and blood. The mongols prepared *borts*, or dried meat, for winter. They made borts from goat, cow, and camel meat.

Milk comes from cattle, goats, sheep, and horses. The

BORTS RECIPE

- With an adult, cut meat in to strips about 11.8 inches (30 cm) long and 2 inches (5 cm) thick. Remove the fat.
- Hang the meat strips in a dry room for 4 to 5 months.
- Cut the dried meat into small pieces.
- Meat will double in size if soaked in water. After soaking, cook the meat for 18 minutes.

Kumiz, or airag, is a popular Mongolian drink. It is made from fermented horse milk.

Mongols make yogurt, cheese, and airag from milk. Airag is so popular among Mongolians, they drink it as often as North Americans drink soda pop.

The Mongols trade for other food items. They combine rice, milk, and brown sugar to make a special holiday food. The Mongols drink tea daily. Salt is one of the few spices the Mongols use for cooking. They eat most meals with either chopsticks or spoons. Although fish is available, Mongols consider it inferior meat. They rarely eat fish. Most wild vegetables are considered food for animals, not humans.

Mongols entertain themselves in many ways. Singing is a popular form of entertainment. A unique singing method called *khoomi* combines sounds from the throat, tongue, nose, and mouth at the same time. The Mongols perform music with instruments such as the morin-khuur, the *limbe*, or bamboo flute, and the *yatag*, an instrument featuring up to fourteen strings. One famous dance, *Bielgee*, or "Dance of the Body," uses just head and hand movements because it was traditionally performed in small yurts.

One children's game is "catching horses," in which boys try to lasso wild horses. Another game, played on ice, is similar to ice hockey and involves kicking an ox anklebone. In "shooting bones," players use a special plank to shoot lamb anklebones at a target.

Great Ideas

During Genghis Khan's rule, Mongol warriors were considered the best of all warriors. Battle by battle, these soldiers dramatically increased the size of the Mongolian Empire. The Mongolian army was trained, disciplined, and organized.

Every Mongol boy was a potential soldier. He grew up learning to ride horses and shoot a bow and arrow. Future warriors practiced killing wild animals. They also gained experience when rival tribes fought over land or horses.

The Mongols knew a great deal about warfare **technology**. Stealing secrets from the Chinese, they learned to melt metals and make weapons. They used swords, **javelins**, axes, **battering rams**, and giant **catapults** that hurled rocks and trees to break enemy walls.

Still, bows and arrows were the most important weapons. The Mongols used a variety of arrows for different situations. They used some arrows to shoot things in the distance. They used others to set fire to enemy towns. Some arrows were used to scare the enemy with their horrible, howling whistles. The Mongols could shoot arrows while riding on horseback. They brought many horses to battles so they could keep riding even after one horse became tired.

Even the clothing the Mongols wore was an

Mongolia has a long military history. Today, each Mongolian man between the ages of 18 and 28 is required to serve in the military for 1 year.

advantage in battle. While European knights were well protected behind heavy armor, they could barely move. The Mongols, on the other hand, wore lighter, more flexible leather armor with metal plates. They hid behind small leather shields. The Mongols also wore silk undershirts. Arrows could not pierce the strong, silk fabric. The silk prevented arrows from making large wounds. A wounded soldier could simply pull the silk out of the wound, bringing the arrow with the fabric.

PORTABLE HOUSES

The yurt, which is also called a *ger*, is a felt tent. This tent is one of the Mongols's best inventions. The yurt protects the Mongols from heat and cold, and it is easy to carry from camp to camp. To set up a yurt, the Mongols make a frame of wooden poles tied together with rope. Then, they stretch felt over the frame. They grease the felt to make it wind- and waterproof. The yurt has a flap door facing south to keep out the cold north winds. The mongols build a fire in the middle of the tent. The fire is surrounded by items such as a stove, beds, tables, chairs, and storage chests. When the Mongols move to a new camp, the yurt is dismantled and taken to the new location on a cart pulled by oxen, camels, or horses.

At Issue

When the Mongolian government became communist, the Mongols's traditional nomadic lifestyle began to decline. Government-run ranches were introduced. Much livestock was taken away from private owners and placed on these ranches. The ranches also used land where the nomads lived. Industry, such as mining and forestry, became more important. Many Mongolians moved into towns or cities to work in factories. When Mongolia became a democracy, many of these factories closed, leaving people without jobs. Today, unemployment is still an issue in Mongolia. Many of the people affected no longer know how to live as nomads.

Still, both herders and businesspeople are important to modern Mongolia. Industry includes manufacturing and construction, from furniture and glass to processed foods. The country now benefits from thousands of privately run businesses. For example, the Mongolian forests supply wood for construction and fuel, and wild animals are

Today, many Mongolians live in apartments in cities such as Ulaanbaatar. Some people build fences around their yurts or live in yurt suburbs surrounding major cities.

hunted for fur and meat. Some of the items Mongolians mine include coal, copper, gold, iron, and petroleum.

The country is one of the world's top producers of **cashmere**. Cashmere, like many items, is **exported** to countries such as Russia and China.

Roads now criss-cross the country, and permanent buildings dot the landscape. About half the Mongolian population lives in towns or cities. In these places, Mongolians often live in concrete apartment buildings. In the suburbs, Mongols still live in yurts. They build fences around the yurts so they can be assigned a house number and receive services such as electricity and mail delivery.

TODAY'S HERDER

Less than half of the Mongolian population continues to live as nomads. Many Mongolian herders now work on large ranches. These ranches are so large they have their own central towns, which offer services such as schools, movie theaters, gas stations, stores, and medical offices. Although horses are still used for transportation, trucks, jeeps, and motorcycles now carry farmers to their herds. Radios offer the latest weather reports, and portable **generators** provide electricity to yurts. Mongolians raise more than 30 million animals, which is greater than the population of Canada. Nearly half of these animals are sheep, which are raised for their meat, milk, furs, and hides. Many of these products are exported.

Into the Future

To learn more about new technology, Mongols stress the benefits of education. At one time, most Mongolian children were uneducated and only taught a few chants and prayers in monasteries. Today, children ages 6 to 16 must attend school. There are 76 universities and colleges, both government-run and privately owned, in which about 130,000 students learn subjects such as agriculture, economics, or medicine.

The Mongolian government has placed special emphasis on teaching its citizens to read. Today, about 90 percent of Mongolians are literate, or able to read. By comparison, about 20 percent of adults in the United States cannot read well enough to understand a food label. In response to the program's success, the country was awarded a **UNESCO** Golden Medal in the 1970s.

The population is also becoming healthier. Poor habits, such as drinking dirty water and not bathing, spread diseases, including smallpox, plague, and diphtheria. Mongols are being taught how to take better care of themselves. They are also learning how to properly care for their babies and the elderly. Enhanced **sanitation** and medical facilities are also improving health. The average Mongol now lives to 65 years of age, and the number of infant deaths has greatly decreased.

In Mongolia, more girls attend school than boys. Many boys in rural areas leave school to work as herders.

The government also encourages families to have more children. This increase in births, combined with the decrease in deaths, has resulted in a huge population surge. In 1900, there were only about 500,000 Mongolians. Today, there are about 2.4 million Mongolians. The population is extremely young. The average Mongol is 21 years of age, and 70 percent of Mongols are younger than 35 years of age.

Tourism is also benefiting the country. Tourists take advantage of the spectacular landscape—including 13 nature reserves—by mountain climbing, skiing, riding, and hiking. They also visit museums to learn about the Mongols's fascinating culture and history.

Historic sites, such as Gandan Monastery, connect Mongols with their past as they move into the future.

BETTER EDUCATION PROGRAMS

After years of changes and upgrades to the education system, most Mongolian children are receiving a proper education. With the fall of the **socialist** government in Mongolia, education funding was greatly reduced. This resulted in cuts to teacher salaries, few building repairs, school closures, and limited textbooks.

In 1996, the Asian Development Bank (ADB) granted Mongolia $6.5 million to improve the quality of the school system. Today, teachers are well paid and resources are widely available. Since 1999–2000, school enrollment has increased to more than 90 percent. In 2002, the Second Education Development Project was approved. The Mongolia government set aside $4.7 million for the project. The ADB provided an additional $14 million, while the government of Japan offered $45 million and the Nordic Development Fund contributed $4.8 million. This project continues to build better school systems and provide better education to all of Mongolia's youth.

Fascinating Facts

- Dinosaur eggs were first discovered in the Gobi Desert.

- A yurt weighs about 550 pounds (250 kilograms), the weight of about three grown men.

- The Gobi bear is the only bear in the world that lives in a desert. Other Gobi animals include the Mongolian wild horse, Asiatic wild donkeys, and wild camels.

- Mongols use items they find in nature, such as manure, which they use as fuel for cooking and heating.

- The Mongols's two-humped Bactrian camels, which they use to carry items when moving, can live up to 3 months on water alone.

- Mongolia did not develop its current form of **currency**, the tögrög, until 1924.

- Mongol horsemen sometimes put raw meat under their saddles. When their day of riding is over, the meat is tender enough to eat.

- Mongolians drink more than 2 million gallons (7.6 million liters) of airag each year.

- In the past, Mongols took their last name from a male ancestor. However, these family names were banned. Today, many people only have a first name and cannot trace their ancestry.

- Nomads and their herds spend the summer on high, flat plains. They spend winters in warmer, sheltered river valleys.

FURTHER READING

Pang, Guek-Cheng. *Mongolia: Cultures of the World*. New York: Marshall Cavendish, 1999.

Reynolds, Jan. *Mongolia: Vanishing Cultures*. New York: Harcourt Brace & Company, 1994.

WEB SITES

Mongolia Today www.mongoliatoday.com

Oyunbilig's Great Mongol Home Page www.mongols.com/index_old.htm

Glossary

archery the activity of shooting with bows and arrows

battering rams huge tree trunks used to break down doors and walls during war

branding marking an animal's skin with a hot iron; done to help identify the animal's owner

bridles leather straps placed over a horse's head

Buddhism a form of religion based on the teachings of Buddha

bureaucrats people who help administer the government

cashmere a fabric made from the soft wool of a goat

catapults machines that can throw large objects

clans groups of people who have a common ancestor

communist a system of government in which one party holds power and the state controls the economy

contiguous neighboring

currency a country's system of money

democratic a system of government in which the citizens elect the leaders

dialects related languages that have slight differences in vocabulary, grammar, or pronunciation

exported selling items to other countries

flint a type of rock used to make a spark to light fires

foreign of or from another country

generators machines used to make electricity

javelins long, pointed weapons

jockeys people who ride racehorses

livestock animals raised for food or other products

mares adult female horses

Mongolian Empire an area uniting nearly all of eastern and western Asia that was ruled by the Mongol khans in the thirteenth and fourteenth centuries

mutton the meat of a sheep

needlework any craft involving decorating with thread and needle

parliament the group of people who run the government

purify to rid of impurities; cleanse

sanitation anything having to do with health and hygiene

scrupulous having principles

silk fabric made from the fine fiber silkworms produce to make cocoons

slaughtered killed an animal for food

socialist a government system that has control of the production and distribution of all goods

steppes large, often treeless, grass-covered plains

stirrups rings hung from a horse's saddle that provide support for the rider's foot

superstitious believing that certain actions can bring good or bad luck

technology scientific discoveries that aid everyday life

telegraph a method of long-distance communication in which coded messages are sent by wire using electricity

titan somebody whose skill is extraordinarily impressive

troops groups of soldiers

UNESCO the United Nations Educational, Scientific, and Cultural Organization

Index

Photograph Credits

Every reasonable effort has been made to trace ownership and to obtain permission to reprint copyright material. The publishers would be pleased to have any errors or omissions brought to their attention so that they may be corrected in subsequent printings.

Cover: Michal Cerny; **Michal Cerny:** pages 1, 3, 5, 6B, 7T, 8B, 10B, 11B, 12B, 13T, 13B, 15, 19B, 21R, 22M, 23, 28B, 29T, 30; **Heather C. Hudak:** page 22B; ©**WOLFGANG KAEHLER 2005** www.wkaehlerphoto.com: pages 7B, 11T, 18B, 20B, 21L, 24B, 25, 26B; **Werner Forman/ Art Resource, NY:** page 14B; **Nik Wheeler/Saudi Aramco World/PADIA:** pages 4T, 6T, 6B, 8T, 10T, 12T, 14T, 16, 17, 18T, 19T, 20T, 22T, 24T, 26T, 27, 28T, 29B; **Mary Evans Picture Library/Explorer/Namur:** page 9.

On the cover
Many Mongols are young people. More than 70 percent of Mongolia's population is under 35 years of age.